All of My Pieces

By E.B. Allen

DEDICATION

Once again, I find myself sitting down to write a dedication to my brilliant daughter, Claire. Her entire life has been this amazing joy that I am lucky enough to have been a part of watching. Sometimes I get a front row seat and other times, like her recent trip to Japan, I have to watch from afar. No matter where her journey takes her, I hope that she always knows her own mind will take her as far as she can imagine.

CONTENTS

Acknowledgments i

1   All of My Pieces   1

2   About the author   97

ACKNOWLEDGMENTS

I would like to acknowledge all of the strangers on both Twitter and Instagram who have given my words a place in this world. Without your support and kindness, I am not sure I would have had the courage to write the first book, let alone this second one here. Thank you all so much for being so amazing

THE DARKNESS INSIDE

Sometimes my mind is very dark and stormy. My thoughts are deeply mysterious, even to myself. Words flow through me. My pen is merely a vessel to which the paper gives an outlet. Like lightening striking. Often it only happens once. If the words are not written down, they will be lost forever. Or perhaps given to another person in the universe. I write because I need to. I crave to get things out of me. This darkness I often feel cannot be contained. My words may be dark sometimes, but my mind is beautiful, and always full of hope.

- MY DARK FRIEND –

CAN YOU HEAR ME, MY DARK FRIEND?
THE DARKNESS HAS BEGUN ONCE AGAIN
NO MORE SILENCE, NO MORE CALM
TEARING DOWN MY WALLS AROUND ME
I CRY OUT LOOKING TO BE SAVED
NO ONE HEARS, NO ONE CARES
DARE TO PEEK OUTSIDE
DYING TO SEE THE LIGHT

-        BREATH   -

I FEEL YOUR BREATH
STANDING BEHIND ME
I WANT TO RUN
HIDE AWAY IN THE SILENCE
STILLNESS TAKES MY HAND
LEAVE ME ALONE, LET ME BE
ESCAPE INTO THE DARKEST PART
JUST LET ME GO, LET ME BE
BUT I STILL FEEL YOUR BREATH
STANDING RIGHT BEHIND ME
I RUN, YOU FOLLOW
NO ESCAPE IN THIS SILENCE
YOU'RE STILL THERE
GRABBING AND PIERCING MY HEART
STABBING THROUGH THE DARKEST HOUR
RESTING AGAINST MY SKIN
I FEEL YOUR BEATING HEART
ONCE AGAIN YOU WIN HERE

-    YOUR MADNESS   -

I'M GONNA RENOUNCE THE MOON TONIGHT
'CAUSE I'M FEELING THE STING OF THE
SWELLING
RUSHING IN AND BUSTING OUT
I'M GONNA LEAVE YOU HERE AND NOW

A RED BIRD CLAWING AT MY WINDOW
CLAMBERING TO GET IN
INVOLVED IN MY MYSTERIES WITHIN

THE HOPE OF LOVE FAILS TO CLIMB
INSIDE THIS BODY
I'M DYING
I'M CRYING
I'M LYING
LYING TO MYSELF THAT ANY OF THIS EVEN
MATTERS

OUT REACHING MY ARMS OF SADNESS
BUT YOUR ANGER BURIES ME WHOLE
TAKING ME ON A RIDE OUTSIDE MY DREAMS
FALLING… FALLING…
FAILING TO REACH ME BEFORE I GO

STOP THIS MADNESS NOW

BLAME YOUR PAIN ON ME
SENDING ME AWAY
YOU TAKE THE BLUE BIRDS VOICE

INTO THE OBLIVION BENEATH MY SOUL
YOU HAUNT MY EVERY MOVE
THEN YOU BRING ME TO MY KNEES

ON MY DARKEST NIGHTS
WHERE WERE YOU FOR ME?
YOUR PRESENCE WAS ALIVE BESIDE ME
BUT MIND AND HEART
THEY WERE NOWHERE TO BE FOUND

YOU CLOSED OFF YOUR WORLD
NOW LET ME SHOW YOU MINE
A TUMBLING MESS OF IDIOSYNCRASIES
WRAPPING THEMSELVES AROUND MY NECK

CLAMBERING TO GET OUT OF THIS MESS
DECIDING TO LOVE YOU STILL
BUT BEING TURNED AWAY
AGAIN
AND AGAIN
AND AGAIN

YOU MOCK MY REASONS
YOU TAINT MY SOUL
YOU TURNED YOUR HEAD
SO I LET GO

- DARK EDGE –

YOUR DARK EDGES CREP INTO MY SOUL
PLAYING WITH MY DEMONS
FROLICKING IN THE SHADOWS
CREATING CREATURES NEVER TO BE
DESTROYED

NO BLOSSOM ON YOUR LIPS
POISONOUS FEELING FINGERTIPS
HORROR STORIES FILL MY HEART
YOUR NASTINESS HAS BECOME AN ART
SENDING DARKNESS THROUGH MY VEINS
IT'S MY HEART THAT NEVER GAINS
LOST ALONE I SIT IN SILENCE
SURROUNDED BY ALL YOUR VIOLENCE

- BRUISED –
DARKNESS FEEDS ME
INGESTING SHADOWS
HEARTS OF BLOOD
CUTS DEEP OPEN
SPRAWLING BRUISES HERE

- CHOKED BREATH -

I AM NOT HERE
NOT WHERE I WANT TO BE
BLEEDING AND BROKEN
BY YOUR MISERY
GRASPING AT THE SWOLLEN AIR
THICK LIKE SMOKE
CHOKING AS I TRY TO BREATHE
CRAWLING TOWARDS ESCAPE
REACHING FOR SOMETHING FAMILIAR
NOTHING BUT HAZE AND DARKNESS
AS I COLLAPSE UNDER YOUR FISTS

-       FEED ME NOISE   –

NO WI-FI
NO MUSIC
NO SOUND
I SIT HERE IN SILENCE
THAT EMPTINESS SURROUNDS MY EVERY
NERVE
MY EVERY FIBER CRIES OUT FOR NOISE
MY MIND COMPETES FOR SUBJECTS
TO DROWN OUT THE SILENCE THAT
ENRAPTURES ME
THAT EMPTINESS THAT IMPALES ME
AS I SIT HERE IN SILENCE

SLOWLY KILLING MY WORLD
FEED ME PILLS OF ENDLESS NOISE
TO DROWN OUT ALL THE PAIN
GIVE ME REASONS TO PUSH THROUGH
THIS CHAOS IS INSANE

- DO NOT ENTER –

TO ENTER HERE
WOULD BE MADNESS
BLINDING
CHAOTIC
MADNESS
YOU MUST WAIT
UNTIL THE DARKNESS PASSES

\-   SECRETS IN MY BONES   -

MY BONES HOLD MANY OF YOUR SECRETS
THESE VEINS HAVE BLED FOR YOU
THE DEPTHS OF MY BEING HAUNT ME
KNOWING EXACTLY WHO YOU REALLY ARE
NO ONE WOULD EVER BELIEVE ME
IF I DESCRIBED YOUR TRUE FACE
YOU CAN HARDLY SEE THE SEEMS
THAT ATTACHES THE MASK YOU WEAR
YOUR STITCHING IS MUCH PRETTIER
THEN THE SCARS I BARE
MY BONES WILL CARRY YOUR SECRETS
TILL THE DAY I DIE

-      DRIFTING AWAY   -

I FEEL LIKE A FEATHER
DRIFTING THROUGH THE WIND
BEING BLOWN AROUND
AND STEPPED ON
THEN PICKED BACK UP AGAIN
I'VE DRIFTED SO FAR AWAY
I NO LONGER RECOGNIZE MYSELF
MY SURROUNDINGS ARE COLD
AND FULL OF DARKNESS
MY COLORS DULL AND GREY
AM I STILL A FEATHER
IF ALL I WAS HAS BEEN TORN AWAY?

WHAT DESTROYED ME IS THE LIES
I CAN HANDLE THE TRUTH
IT MAY HURT FOR A BIT
BUT I'LL GET OVER IT
THE UNKNOWN HURTS FOREVER
DECEPTION CREATES A FEAR
AN UNTRUSTING WAY OF LIFE
THAT'S ALL I'VE COME TO KNOW

- FLY AWAY WITH ME –

I COULD FLY AWAY WITH NOTHING BUT YOU
BY MY SIDE
TAKE ON THE WORLD WITH NOTHING BUT
YOUR HAND IN MINE
AND SEEK OUT THE ANSWERS OF THE
UNIVERSE
WITH NOTHING BUT YOUR LOVE TO GUIDE ME

-        COME CLOSER   -

COME CLOSE
TO ME
BRING ME CLOSER
THAN BEFORE
BRING ME CLOSER
THE WHOLE NIGHT THROUGH
MAKE ME A BELIEVER
IN SOMETHING MAGICAL
COME CLOSER

-   THE UNIVERSE   –

THE UNIVERSE HAS A CRUEL SENSE OF HUMOR
GIVING US EXACTLY WHAT WE ASKED FOR
BUT AT TOTALLY THE WRONG TIME

-        LOVING YOU   –

THERE SEEMS TO BE MORE OF ME
LOVING YOU
THAN THERE WILL EVER BE OF YOU
LOVING ME

-      NO FEAR   –

THERE IS A VIOLENCE
CREEPING UP QUICKLY
HIDDEN BEHIND
THOSE DARK EYES
AND A WHIMSICAL SMILE
I SHOULD FEAR
SOMETHING ABOUT YOU
BUT HERE I AM
NOT BACKING DOWN

-       FADING AWAY   –

FADING AWAY
INTO AN OBLIVION
JUST PAST THE PALE
WHERE THE FOREST
MEETS THE WATER'S EDGE
TAKE A MOMENT
BEFORE YOU TAKE THE PLUNGE
INTO THE DARKNESS
THAT AWAITS UNDERNEATH IT ALL

- YOUR HANDS -

YOUR HANDS FEEL LIKE AN OLD SONG
A SLOW MELODY GLIDING THROUGH MY VEINS
YOUR LIPS HITTING ALL THE HIGH NOTES
SINGING OUT ACROSS MY ENTIRE BODY
THE CHORUS MAKING ME BEG FOR MORE
TIME AND TIME AGAIN

- TAKE MY HAND –

TAKE MY HAND
BEFORE THE DARKNESS
LEADS ME BACK
INTO THE NIGHT
KISS ME HARDER
SO I CAN ESCAPE
THE MADNESS INSIDE
PULL ME CLOSER
DON'T EVER LET ME GO

-        PULLING ME IN   –

THE DARKNESS IS PULLING ME IN
CLOSER THAN BEFORE
HAUNTING ME WITH ITS TEMPTATIONS
OF UNDERSTANDING ME MORE THAN ANYONE
ELSE
GRABBING ME TIGHTER THAN LAST TIME
LEADING ME ONTO A PATH
WHERE I PROBABLY BELONG

- TOMORROW FADING –

TOMORROW IS FADING QUICKLY
WITH EVERY HOUR OF TODAY
TICK, TICK, TICKING BY
I'M WALKING OUT ON DREAMS
OF YESTERDAY
FOR THINGS I'M FEELING TODAY

- FALLING SIDEWAYS –

I HAVE FALLEN SIDEWAYS
THROUGH THE DARKNESS
I CAN NO LONGER
CLOSE MY EYES
THERE IS A MADNESS
WAITING FOR ME TO BREAK
AND FALL SILENT
AGAINST THE NIGHT

-      MY BROKEN SOUL   —

DO YOU FEEL MY BROKEN SOUL
WHEN YOU TOUCH MY SKIN
CAN YOU FEEL MY SHARPNESS
THE EDGES THAT FALL AWAY
A LITTLE BIT MORE EACH DAY
CAN YOU SEE THE PILES OF ASH
BENEATH MY FEET
FROM ALL THE FIRES
BURNING INSIDE ME
CAN YOU SEE THE DARKNESS
THAT HAUNTS ME
WHEN YOU LOOK IN MY EYES

- IN MY BED –

STAY HERE IN BED WITH ME
LET THE THUNDER DROWN OUT MY VOICE
AS I BEG YOU FOR MORE
STAY HERE IN BED WITH ME
JUST ONE MORE TIME
DON'T LET THIS NIGHT END

-      SCREAM AT THE NIGHT   –

I WOULD SCREAM AT THE SKY
IF I THOUGHT THAT WOULD HELP
THE MADNESS OF IT ALL
I DID THIS TO MYSELF
I CREATED THE MONSTER
THAT NOW SITS INSIDE
EATING AWAY AT MY SOUL

I TRIED CLIMBING INTO YOUR WORLD
SUCH A LONG WAY UP
THE HIGHER I GOT
THE MORE I FEARED LOSING YOU
SO I LET GO
IT'L BE A LONG ROAD TO RECOVERY
AFTER A FALL LIKE THIS
SUCH A LONG WAY DOWN
CRASHING INTO THE GROUND

-        YOUR HANDS -

YOUR HANDS
BELONG
IN PLACES
NO ONE
GETS TO SEE
TOUCH
MY FLESH
HOLD
ME TIGHTLY
DEEP
INTO THE NIGHT

\-   I TRY TO LOVE   –

I TRY TO LOVE
BUT LOVE ISN'T
ALWAYS FAIR
NOT TO ME
ANYWAY
I TRY TO LOVE
BUT FIND
THERE IS NO ONE
SENDING ME LOVE
BACK
I TRY TO LOVE
BUT END UP HURTING
OVER FEELINGS
I SHOULD HAVE NEVER GIVEN
AWAY

- FORGOTTEN –

IT ISN'T THAT I HAVE FORGOTTEN HOW TO BREATHE
OR THAT I HAVE FORGOTTEN HOW TO SPEAK
IT IS THAT THE SECOND YOU ARE NEAR ME
MY MIND WONDERS OFF WITH WILD THOUGHTS
LIKE KISSING YOU EVER SO SLOWLY
WITH YOUR HANDS GRASPING ME FIRMLY

IT ISN'T THAT I NEED YOU TO HELP ME BREATHE
IT IS THAT YOU ARE THE REASON I BEGIN TO AGAIN
ONCE THE THOUGHTS SETTLE AND I AM CENTERED
BY THE IDEA OF YOU BEING MORE THAN JUST THAT
MOMENT
MORE TO ME THAN JUST THIS PASSION

YES, YOU TAKE MY BREATH AWAY
BUT YOU ARE THE REASON I AM BREATHING IN LIFE SO
DEEPLY

- WOULD YOU –

IF I STARTED TO RUN AWAY
WOULD YOU TURN YOUR BACK
WALK OUT AND FORGET
I EVER EXISTED
OR WOULD YOU FIGHT
TO KEEP ME BY YOUR SIDE
AND IN YOUR LIFE
FOREVER
WOULD YOU…
BE THERE FOR ME
IF I NEEDED SOMEONE
TO KEEP ME FROM RUNNING

-       STEAL A MOMENT   -

I WANT TO STEAL A MOMENT
AWAY FROM THE DARKNESS
THAT HAS BEEN CONSUMING
MY WORLD FOR FAR TOO LONG
SINK MY FLESH INTO
LOVING ARMS THAT WRAP
ALL THE WAY AROUND ME
UNTIL I KNOW NOTHING ELSE
I WANT TO STEAL A MOMENT
KNOWING WE CAN NEVER
GET THAT SAME TIME
BACK EVER AGAIN

-            ONLY DARKNESS   –

IF YOU ALLOW YOURSELF TO SEE ONLY
DARKNESS IN ANOTHER PERSON, THEN YOU
ARE MISSING OUT ON ALL OF THEIR LIGHT.

MY DEMONS WOULD EAT YOUR DEMONS FOR
BREAKFAST AND THEN ASK FOR MORE.

-      HEROINE   –

THOUGHTS OF YOU
TWISTING INSIDE ME
LIKE A HIT OF HEROINE
BURNING IN MY VEINS
YOU ARE MY ADDICTION
MY WORDS STRUNG ABOUT
LIKE USED UP NEEDLES
IN A JUNKIES HOUSE
AN UNHEALTHY CRAVING
NEEDING TO BE SATISFIED

-     MEET ME   –

MEET ME
IN DARKNESS
TEMPT ME
WITH KISSES
SWEET
LIKE HONEY
HOT
LIKE SUMMER
FEEL MY
FLESH
PULL ME
CLOSER
FEED MY
SOUL

NO ONE COMPLETES YOU
MAYBE THEY COMPLEMENT YOUR STYLE
OR HELP BALANCE A BIT OF YOUR LIFE
THERE ARE NO MISSING PIECES
YOU ARE AN ENTIRE PERSON
ALL ON YOUR OWN

-   TAKE A CHANCE   –

I AM THE PERSON YOU THINK YOU WANT
BUT THE ONE YOU'LL NEVER TAKE A CHANCE ON

- BREAK ME –

BREAK ME
SO I CAN LAUGH
IN THE FACE
OF THE MADNESS
THAT IS LOVE

-        LOVE   -

I DIDN'T ASK TO LOVE
I WAS BORN TO LOVE
I CRAVE LOVE
NEED LOVE
WANT LOVE
ANY LOVE
ALL LOVE

-        DEVOUR   -

SLIP RIGHT IN
FIND A SPOT
STAY FOR A WHILE
YOUR HANDS
AS A GUIDE
YOUR LIPS
DEVOUR

THE FLESH
OF SINS
TAKE SHAPE
AS BREATH
QUICKENS
DEEPER STILL

AN ENDLESS
JOURNEY
FUELED BY
YOUR HEARTS
DESIRES

-      LESS ME   –

FEELING LESS LIKE MYSELF
AND MORE LIKE A STRANGER
SAME SKIN
DIFFERENT MINDSET
CHANGING THOUGHTS
LIKE A CHAMELEON
MY COLORS RUN WILD
WITH THOUGHTS
NEVER THERE BEFORE
BEGGING TO BE
LET LOOSE

-     BEYOND THE PALE   –

DON'T EXPECT AN ANSWER
NOT BEYOND THE PALE
A MEEK TRIBUTE
TO WHAT LOVE IS
NOT TO BE COMPARED
TO WHAT LOVE ISN'T
THERE IS A VASTNESS
OF VOID TO CONSIDER
IF YOU MUST ASK
THEN NEVER EXPECT
FOR YOU WILL BE
DISAPPOINTED
WITH WHAT LITTLE
THAT TINY MAN
HAS TO OFFER YOU

-     BULLETPROOF   –

I COULD HAVE SWORN I WAS BULLETPROOF
THEN I MET YOU
NOW I'M RIDDLED WITH HOLES
AND DRIPPING BLOOD
POURING MYSELF OUT
ONTO PAGES AND FILM
TRYING TO FILL IN THE EMPTY SPACES
WITH THINGS THAT DISTRACT ME
FROM THE OBVIOUS PAIN
THAT IS THIS HORRIFYING IMAGE
OF WHAT GLANCES BACK AT ME
WHEN I LOOK INTO THE MIRROR
AND SEE WHAT USED TO BE ME
BUT INSTEAD IS A DESTROYED
UNLESS PERSONA OF… YOU

-      I WAITED   –

IT WAS IN THAT BREATH I WAITED
ANXIOUS FOR YOUR KISS
FOR YOU TO GRAB ME
PULL ME IN CLOSER
AND SHOW ME
THAT YOU LOVED ME

IT WAS IN THE BREATH I WAITED
CURIOUS FOR YOU
TO SPEAK YOUR FEELINGS
TELL ME HOW YOU FEEL
AND PROVE I'M NOT ALONE
IN THIS GREAT BIG CRAZY WORLD

IT WAS IN THAT BREATH I WAITED
FOR SOMETHING WONDERFUL
TO FINALLY HAPPEN TO ME
TO FEEL LOVE UPON MY LIPS
AND ONCE AGAIN QUENCH
DESIRES HELD DEEP INSIDE

-     MAYBE, SOMEDAY   –

I'M THROWN BY YOUR DEFINITION
OF MAYBE
AND SOMEDAY
SOMEDAY WAS A WHILE AGO
AND YOU STILL SAY MAYBE
WELL MAYBE ISN'T ANYWHERE
NO SPACE IN TIME I CAN HOLD
NO ARMS TO GRAB ME
NO LIPS TO KISS ME
NO FLESH TO WRAP MYSELF AROUND
JUST EMPTY WORDS
AND PROMISES OF NOTHING

-      LOST   -

I GET LOST IN THE BREATHS
WAITING FOR YOUR LIPS TO REACH MINE
RACING HEARTBEATS
FELT THROUGH YOUR CHEST
AND STRAIGHT INTO MINE
WHILE YOU REST GENTLY
ON TOP OF ME
WITH AN ANTICIPATION
GROWING DEEPER
IN EACH OF OUR MINDS
THOUGHTS UNSPOKEN
YET KNOWN
OUR LIPS FINALLY MEET
AND THERE IS NO STOPPING US NOW

\-   HIDDEN   \-

I WANT TO ENJOY EVERYTHING ABOUT YOU –
EVEN THE PARTS YOU KEEP HIDDEN.

- STAIN MY PAGES –

I LET YOU WRITE YOURSELF INTO MY PAGES
TINY SCRIBBLES OF DARK INK
SOME MAKE SENSE
OTHERS ARE PURE NONSENSE
YOU WILL NEVER BE MORE
THAN INK STAINS ON A PAGE
IN A BOOK
THAT WILL NEVER BE READ AGAIN

- ADDICTED -

MAYBE I'M ADDICTED TO THE PAIN
OR MAYBE IT'S ALL THE PLEASURE BEFORE
EITHER WAY I WANT YOU HERE WITH ME
UNTIL YOU LEAVE ME AGAIN

-   MY FRIENDS -

ALL MY FRIENDS ARE GHOSTS
FROM PASTS
FORGOTTEN
BUT MISSED
DEEPLY
MY SOUL ACHES
THINKING
OF EACH
AND EVERY
FUCKING ONE
OF THEM

- WILD LOVE -

I WANT A WILD LOVE
FROM A GENTLE SOUL
SOMEONE WHO UNDERSTANDS
MY UNIQUELY STRANGE MIND

- MAYBE ONCE -

MAYBE ONCE
I WILL FIND LOVE
WAITING
PERHAPS ONCE
IT WILL STAY
FOREVER
POSSIBLY ONCE
HE WILL DESIRE ME
OFTEN

- ESCAPE -

I NEED TO ESCAPE. AWAY FROM THIS TOWN
AND THESE MEMORIES. I NEED TO START
SOMEWHERE NEW AGAIN. I AM A GYPSY SOUL
STRANDED IN A TOWN WITH NO HEART. I
REQUIRE A BEAT AND A RHYTHM TO MAKE ME
WANT TO STAY. THIS TOWN IS DEAD AND FULL
OF GHOSTS.

- STAINED MY HEART -

YOU'LL BE IN MY HEART
FOREVER
FOR THIS LOSS
HAS STAINED ME
A DEEP SHADE OF BLUE
MY LIPS ARE PERMANENTLY
SWEET FOR YOUR FLESH
MY HANDS WILL ALWAYS
REACH FOR YOU
THIS SOUL OF MINE
IS DARK AND LOST
WITHOUT YOU

- BLEEDING OUT STARS -

I AM AN OPEN TEAR IN THE UNIVERSE.
BLEEDING OUT STARS AND WONDERING WHY
ALL THE LIGHT IS LEAVING ME BEHIND.

- LET ME BREATHE -

JUST LET ME BREATHE
RELEASE YOUR HOLD ON ME
I AM NOT YOURS
I RAN TO HIDE
YOUR FINDING ME
DOESN'T MEAN A THING
I AM FREE
FROM YOU
FROM THAT LIFE
LET ME GO
LET ME BREATHE
SET ME FREE

- NEVER CHANGE -

HE WAS DIFFERENT.
I WANTED DIFFERENT.

I WAS STRANGE.
HE WANTED PERFECT.

I CHANGED FOR HIM.
HE LEFT ME.

MY HEART BROKE.
HIS HEART WAS FINE.

I'M STILL STRANGE.
HE'S STILL DIFFERENT.

I NEED DIFFERENT.
HE NEEDS PERFECT.

* I'LL NEVER CHANGE FOR ANOTHER AGAIN

I FEEL THE WEIGHT OF THE MOON AS IT PULLS
AGAINST THE TIDES. MY SOUL UNDERSTANDS
NEEDING TO REACH SOMETHING SO FAR OUT
OF MY GRASP... BUT STILL TRYING AGAIN AND
AGAIN TO FEEL ITS TOUCH.

SHE HAS SWEETNESS IN HER VEINS, BUT WITH
A SIMPLE TOUCH FROM HIM... IT IS MORE LIKE
GUNPOWDER READY TO IGNITE.

THE TROUBLE WITH BEING COMFORTABLE IN DARKNESS... HORROR FILLED PEOPLE DO NOT FRIGHTEN US AWAY. WE LOVE THEM. THEY HURT US. AND WE JUST BECOME DARKER.

OUR WORLDS COLLIDED UNEXPECTEDLY AND
THEN THEY BURNT DOWN JUST AS
BEAUTIFULLY. THE FIRE FLICKERED OUT INTO
TOTAL DARKNESS. YOU WERE GONE AND MY
SOUL, NOW ASHES, FLOATED AROUND IN A
CHAOTIC STORM SEEKING SOMEONE TO CALM
IT.

I WANT MY LOVE TO SNEAK ITS WAY INTO
YOUR HEART. MAYBE YOU WON'T NOTICE
THAT I AM IMPERFECT OR THAT I AM DARK
AND A LITTLE STRANGE. IF I TIPTOE THROUGH
YOUR VEINS... MAYBE YOU WILL LET ME STAY.

THE MOON SEEMS A MILLION MILES AWAY
TONIGHT BUT THAT'S STILL CLOSER THAN YOU
WILL EVER BE TO ME AGAIN.

-   STRONGER -

I'M OK WITH ALL OF THIS CHAOS AND
DARKNESS BECAUSE IN THE END... I WILL BE
STRONGER, AND YOU WILL NEVER BREAK ME
AGAIN.

- EXHALE YOU -

THE BREATH I TOOK BEFORE WE SAID
GOODBYE THAT LAST TIME... STILL CLINGS TO
MY SOUL. KEEPING ME ALIVE. KEEPING ME IN
LOVE. I'VE TRIED TO EXHALE YOU, BUT YOU
ARE A PART OF ME NOW.

- WAKE ME UP -

WAKE ME UP WHEN THE SHADOWS HAVE
GONE AWAY. THAT'S MY FAVORITE TIME TO
PLAY.

MAYBE I WASN'T MEANT TO LOVE HIM
BUT I DID IT ANYWAY
AND FOR A MOMENT
I FELT ALIVE

YOUR WORDS GENTLY KISS EVERY INCH OF MY
BODY WHENEVER YOU SPEAK. YOU TAKE MY
MIND DEEPER. YOU MAKE ME ACHE FOR YOUR
TOUCH. YOU BRING ME PLEASURE WITHOUT
EVEN KNOWING IT. FEED ME YOUR WORDS
AND I AM YOURS.

- NOT PERFECT -

HIS HANDS WEREN'T PERFECT, BUT THEY HELD
ME TOGETHER WHENEVER I FELL APART. HIS
EYES WEREN'T PERFECT, BUT THEY SAW ME
FOR WHO I WAS IN THIS WORLD. HIS LIPS
WEREN'T PERFECT, BUT THEY KISSED ME
SWEETLY. HIS LIFE WAS NOT PERFECT, BUT IT
FIT IN WITH MINE NICELY.

I EXPERIENCED YOU IN A DEEP BREATH
HIDDEN BENEATH THE DARKNESS. MY SOUL
CARRIED YOU AWAY FOR JUST A MOMENT. I
LOST YOU. BUT I WILL NEVER FORGET YOU.

I ONCE UNDERSTOOD WHY LOVE IS SO
BEAUTIFUL. THEN I MET YOU AND LEARNED
THAT LOVE IS DARK AND PAINFUL.

THE KNIFES EDGE BALANCING ON MY
WEAKENED HEART. SLOWLY SLIPPING DEEPER
WITH EACH BREATH I TAKE TRYING TO
FORGET ABOUT HIM.

-   COCAINE   -

YOU WERE SWEET LIKE HONEY AND I CRAVE
YOU MORE THAN EVER BEFORE, BUT I KNOW
YOU ARE MORE LIKE COCAINE THAN LOVE TO
ME. A EUPHORIC HIGH EVERY FUCKING NIGHT
IN BED...BUT A DEPRESSING LOW THE NEXT
DAY IN YOUR SILENCE. LIKE A DRUG, MY MIND
WILL ALWAYS WANT YOU IN ME.

THERE IS NO CLOSURE IN SILENCE. JUST
FEELINGS OF LOSS THAT LAST FOR A LIFETIME.

- KILLING ME SLOWLY -

IT CREEPS IN SLOWLY. POISONING MY VEINS.
THIS THING YOU CALL LOVE IS KILLING ME
SLOWLY WITH EACH PASSING GLANCE THAT
YOU PLACE UPON MY FLESH.

HE NEVER STOOD A CHANCE TRYING TO BE
WITH A GIRL LIKE ME. A WEAK MIND COULD
NEVER UNDERSTAND WHY LOVE IS
IMPORTANT FOR A POET. WHY FEELING
SOMEONE DEEPER THAN THEIR FLESH MEANS
EVERYTHING. WHY A CONVERSATION ABOUT
NOTHING COULD BE FELT FOR DAYS.

WE BALANCE ALONG THE EDGE OF THE ABYSS
AND WAIT TO FALL IN ONE MORE TIME.

ALL THE POISONOUS SOUNDS THAT FILL OUR
MINDS EACH AND EVERY DAY... I SEARCH FOR
ONE BEAUTIFUL SOUND AND HOLD ONTO IT
THROUGH THE NIGHT.

AS THE LAST BUBBLE OF AIR ESCAPED HER LIPS
AND SHE DRIFTED DEEPER INTO THE ABYSS
HER MIND THOUGHT ONLY OF HIS BEAUTIFUL
LIPS.

- NUMB -

I BECAME USED TO THE WAY YOU NUMBED
ALL MY PAIN. NOW I'M JUST NUMB TO
EVERYTHING SINCE YOU'VE BEEN GONE.

IN THE QUIET DARK SPACES OF WHO I WAS
AND WHO I WANT TO BE... I FOUND SOMEONE
ASKING ME TO BE SOMEONE DIFFERENT. I
LISTENED FOR A WHILE. I TRIED IT THEIR WAY.
MAKE BELIEVE IS FINE... EXCEPT WHEN YOU
ARE ASKING SOMEONE TO LOVE YOU FOR
WHO YOU WANT TO BE.

IT WAS AS IF A STORM CAME THROUGH MY
SOUL AND BLEW AWAY ALL THE PARTS OF YOU
THAT I LOVED... BECAUSE I WOKE UP ONE
MORNING NOT MISSING YOU ANYMORE. AND
ON THAT DAY... MY LIFE BEGAN AGAIN WITH A
FRESH START AT FINDING HAPPINESS.

-   DEPLETED   -

I HAVE BEEN DEPLETED OF ALL THINGS
BEAUTIFUL IN THE SILENCE AND HAVE BEEN
LEFT WITH THIS DARK VOID THAT ECHOES IN
MY EARS.

THE INK SPILLED ACROSS THE PAGE. MY
FINGERS SMUDGING IT. MIXING WORDS
TOGETHER. POETRY BECAME MESSY. AND
MESSY BECAME MY TRUE LOVE.

IT IS TIMES LIKE THIS WHEN THE NIGHT HAS
YET TO BEGIN AND THE SILENCE IS ALREADY
SETTLING IN NICELY... WHERE THE STORIES OF
MY PRIVATE WORLD UNFOLD ONTO THE
PAGES BENEATH MY PEN.

I CAN STILL FEEL THE WEIGHT OF YOUR
BREATH ON MY NECK. COLLAPSING INTO
DARKNESS OF PAIN... I LET IT SINK INSIDE MY
SOUL. AS IF YOU WERE STILL HERE NEXT TO
ME. YOU ARE GONE. BUT THESE MEMORIES
WILL LAST A LIFETIME.

- AWAKENED -

HIS SOUL SEEMED SO SWEET. LIKE FROSTING
ON TOP OF A DELICATE CAKE. UPON TASTING...
THE SOUR AND BITTER TWISTED MESS OF
DARKNESS SPRINKLED WITH LIES CAME
CRASHING DOWN MY THROAT. CHOKING ON
THE CHAOS THAT ALMOST KILLED MY MIND...
EYES CLOSED FOR DAYS.
AWAKENED.

-   WHAT IS RIGHT   -

THE DISTANCE BETWEEN WHAT IS RIGHT
AND WHAT IS WRONG
THE BLOOD WE SHED FIGHTING
STANDING UP FOR THOSE WITHOUT A VOICE
IN THE END WE WILL UNDERSTAND LOVE
CONQUERS ALL THAT IS EVIL
AND THE DARKNESS WILL FADE AWAY
LEAVING WHAT IS PURE
RESTING ON THE TIP OF OUR FINGERS

BETWEEN THE TIME OF FOREVER AND
NOTHING
A MOMENT WAITS
WITH A BEATING HEART SEEKING
ANSWERS FROM WITHIN
A TOUCH BECOMES MORE
THEN ONE REALIZES
FROM A BREATH THAT WAS STOLEN
THERE IS ONLY ONE ANSWER

COULD HE BE THE ONE
WHO SAVES A BROKEN SOUL

WE DO NO SEEK OUT THE WORDS CLAWING AT OUR VEINS. THEY FIND US IN THE MOST PECULIAR OF WAYS. BEGGING US TO WRITE THEM DOWN.

- UNDERSTAND HER -

TO UNDERSTAND HER HEART, YOU WILL NEED
TO LET GO OF EVERYTHING YOU THINK YOU
KNOW ABOUT YOURSELF. SHE WILL MAKE YOU
FEEL THINGS YOU NEVER THOUGHT WERE
POSSIBLE.

- SHE IS -

SHE IS PURE POETRY. BREATHE IN AND FEEL
HER HEAL YOUR BROKEN SOUL.

LETTING GO OF PIECES THAT ONCE HELD ME
TOGETHER. NEVER TO BE WHOLE AGAIN. I GO
FORWARD WITH ALL THAT'S LEFT OF ME.
FORGETTING ALL ABOUT THE PIECES YOU
STOLE FROM ME.

ABOUT THE AUTHOR

EB Allen started writing poetry as more than just for homework when a teacher wrote "see me after class" on a poetry assignment in 10th grade. The teacher said it was like nothing they had ever seen before. He encouraged her to keep writing poetry. She has been writing ever since then. It has given her an outlet to heal through many traumatic experiences in her life. Something that she feels very lucky to have been given; a way to cope with things that many others have also gone through in life. She hopes that her words help others heal too.

www.ingramcontent.com/pod-product-compliance
Lightning Source LLC
Chambersburg PA
CBHW020553030426
42337CB00013B/1080